Quality Service Pure and Simple

A Primer for Improving Service in Your Organization

Quality Service
Pure and Simple

*A Primer for Improving Service in
Your Organization*

by
Ronald W. Butterfield

Quality Service Pure and Simple

Ronald W. Butterfield

Library of Congress Cataloging-in-Publication Data
Butterfield, Ronald W.
    Quality service pure and simple : a primer for
improving service in your organization / by
Ronald W. Butterfield.
        p. cm.
    Includes bibliographical references and index.
    ISBN 0-87389-091-4
    1. Service industries—Quality control.
I. Title.
HD9980.5.B83   1991
658.8'12—dc20   90-39254
                                              CIP

Acquisitions Editor: Jeanine L. Lau
Production Editor: Tammy Griffin
Cover design by Wayne Dober.
Set in Century Schoolbook by Carlisle Communications, Ltd.
Printed and bound by Edwards Brothers.

Printed in the United States of America
10987654321

**ASQC Quality Press, American Society for Quality Control
310 West Wisconsin Avenue, Milwaukee, Wisconsin 53203**

TABLE OF CONTENTS

OVERVIEW

No matter what business or occupation you're in, service is an integral part of what you do. Organizations that realize service means "customer focused"—not just at the front line but throughout the entire work force—have a significant strategic advantage. Service is a planned, systematic means of providing for the wants, needs, and desires of your customers.

The good news is that customers will pay more for what they perceive to be higher quality or more reliable service. Service is an excellent way to distinguish your organization from your competitors, but don't promise more than you can deliver. The secret to successfully using service as a marketing tool is to build high expectations in the minds of your customers *after* you have developed a service delivery system that allows you to consistently meet those expectations.

Chapter 3:   Defining Service for Your Organization **17**

Assumption is the lowest form of knowledge.
Never assume you know what the customer wants.
Service can only be defined from the customers'
perspective and you can only find out what customers think by asking them. Customer feedback
can be obtained in several fairly simple and inexpensive ways including: focus groups, telephone
surveys, mail surveys, and suggestion boxes. (Sam-
pling and designing simple questionnaires are also
covered.)

Chapter 4:   Measuring Service Performance   **27**

You'll never know if you're winning the service
game without a scorecard. You need a reliable
means of measuring performance all the way down
to the individual employee level. There should be
key measures for both internal and external performance indicators. Internal measures focus on
the organizational view of how you're doing. External measures gauge customer perceptions. Internal measures should include volumes, accuracy,
productivity, timeliness, backlogs, and unit cost.
External measures help you get a feel for the level
of customer satisfaction that can be attributed to
the various components of a product or service.

Chapter 5:   What Not to Do   **35**

Service improvement, like any major organizational initiative, is fraught with pitfalls to be
avoided. Fourteen examples of the most common
implementation errors made by management are
included in this chapter. The underlying message
is that respect for the individual, good two-way
communication, and a well-thought-out plan mixed

with a little humility are the keys to implementing a successful service improvement process. You can't do it alone. You and your employees must work together.

The five principles of service discussed in this chapter are: 1) pay attention to the little things; 2) conduct business by the golden rule; 3) understand your customers; 4) encourage innovation, and 5) value your people.

Nothing is more important to an organization's success than the employee's ability to communicate with customers. There are many key elements involved in the communication process—over 90 percent of it is via non-verbal channels. Non-verbal communication includes tone of voice, facial expression, and body language. The biggest mistake many organizations make is to assume employees know how to communicate effectively. The time and money spent developing your staff's communication skills are two of the best investments you'll ever make.

Whether an organization has one employee or 100,000, the process of implementing a service strategy is identical. The challenge for each organization lies in how well its people can execute the nine implementation steps described in this chapter.

INTRODUCTION

Have you read all the "excellence" books that tell you how poor service is in the United States and then present dozens of anecdotes about companies that do it right? If you're like most people who are interested in the subject of service, you probably bought at least a few of those books and have them resting on your bookshelf or in your briefcase with a bookmark in Chapter 3 that hasn't moved in months. You know that service is truly important, but just can't manage to wade through all those books.

Why can't you finish reading those books? I think there are two reasons: information overload and a lack of time. In addition, some texts are just plain disappointing in their how-to content.

Hence the reason for this book. Service is *the* competitive edge. Realizing the value of time in U.S. society, I've tried to compress 15 years of observation and work in the service end of various organizations into a primer which illustrates how to improve service in any organization. This book is designed to pinpoint specific steps that are part of any successful improvement effort, and it details pitfalls to avoid. It's designed to stimulate your thinking—something many of us do too little of because we're so busy fighting fires.

What you will read here is neither highly technical nor complex. Much of the presentation is just good old common sense. The book outlines simple methods and practices that have proven their value time and again, but sometimes it takes a little prodding to return to the basics.

This book was written as a service to you, the reader. Your comments are important to me. Please send them to:

Ron Butterfield
c/o ASQC Quality Press
310 West Wisconsin Avenue
Milwaukee, Wisconsin 53203

Best wishes as you strive to make service the competitive edge for your organization.

Are You in a Service Business?

Service is a system of satisfactorily providing for the wants, needs, and desires of clients, patients, or customers. It is work performed in an established and orderly way on behalf of others.

If you're in any business, government, or nonprofit organization, service is your business. Whether you manufacture electronic components, publish clients' books, repair automobiles, sell real estate, sell retail groceries, run a hospital, cut hair, guide fishing expeditions, or are the town mayor, service is an integral part of what you do.

Service is a system of satisfactorily providing for the wants, needs, and desires of clients, patients, or customers. It is work performed in an established, orderly way on behalf of others. Unfortunately, until recently, many organizations have not given much thought to the concept of service. It is usually assumed that the service is OK if customers register few complaints. This factor has been especially true of successful enterprises. Prosperity has a way of hiding the weaknesses of a business, but prosperity seldom continues without careful and constant thought on management's part. That careful thought uncovers and provides remedies for the organization's weaknesses.

Sometimes complacency with the status quo can be shattered only by outside forces. Consumerism, increasing competition, and an erratic economy have made it necessary for virtually all organizations to reexamine relationships with customers. Companies are beginning to recognize the strategic value of superior service as a powerful force in boosting sales. They are realizing that the quality of each contact with the customer is escalating in importance.

In an increasingly impersonal, high-tech society, customers want to feel they are more than just a sale. The GE commercial that promises, "We don't desert you after we deliver it," is an effort to soothe the fears of customers who have experienced the "You bought it; it's your problem" syndrome.

Consider the following three examples taken from personal experience:

One evening my family of five went out for dinner at a fast-food establishment which had been in operation for a couple of years. Two of the dinner orders we received were burned, yet the food was cold by the time we got it. The other three orders of ground beef burritos literally dripped puddles of grease on their plates. Even the orange soda was flat and it had anything but an orange flavor. The meal was a disaster, to say the least. Our first clue that trouble was on the horizon should have been when we noticed there were only two employees in the store and only one other customer during what should have been rush hour.

The following day my wife wrote a polite but honest letter to the store manager describing what had happened. In less than a week she received a nice letter of apology from the manager and including coupons for free meals approximating the cost of what we had purchased. The event had a happy ending, right? Wrong. The evening of the day we received the letter and coupons, we drove past the restaurant and guess what we saw? The sign that usually displayed the day's specials read "Closed. For Lease." Evidently we weren't the only ones to experience the establishment's culinary delights and extraordinary service.

Now to relate the second experience involving a well-known, highly respected hotel in Chicago. I checked in to the hotel on a Sunday night. The registration desk clerks and the bellman were polite and helpful. The room was clean and nicely appointed.

I spent the following day in business meetings outside the hotel. When I returned that evening, I noticed that my electric razor was missing from where I had left it on the bathroom vanity. I searched the room to see if anything else was missing, but only the razor was gone.

I called the security officer on duty. He came to my room and carefully listened to my story, then he filled out a statement of loss form and asked me to sign it. He told me they would conduct an investigation and that they should be able to inform me of the results by the time I was scheduled to check out later in the week.

At checkout time I inquired as to the hotel's progress on the case. Nothing had turned up but I was informed that they would continue the investigation. I was given the name and number of the security director and the hotel manager and instructed to call them if I didn't hear from them within two weeks. Three weeks later I called the manager. He said they had not been able to find anything that would help them determine what had happened to the razor. I then asked him what would happen if the razor was not found within a reasonable period of time. He politely informed me that they had "no mechanism for handling the loss of items valued at less than $100 after 60 days has elapsed." (Obviously this implies that if you are going to travel, you should make sure your electric razor is worth at least $100.)

Well, 60 days passed and I heard nothing so I sat down and wrote a letter to the hotel chain's chairman. I explained what had happened and told him I felt I should be reimbursed $35 for the estimated value of the lost razor.

Within a few days I received his response explaining that my letter had been forwarded to the hotel manager for handling and that if I didn't hear from him within 10 days I should contact the chairman's office again. Apparently the letter got the wheels of progress rolling because the following week I received a check for $35 and a letter apologizing for the inconvenience. My faith in the hotel was restored and I will not hesitate to return there now that the problem was resolved satisfactorily.

The final illustration of personal consumer frustration involves my family's experience in purchasing kitchen floor covering and having it installed by "professionals."

After buying our current home and preparing to move in, we found that the existing flooring had been damaged while the previous owners were moving out. Of course the seller blamed the moving company and the moving company blamed the seller so we ended up being stuck with the problem.

Being on a rather tight budget, we shopped carefully for the best price on the purchase and installation of high quality, name brand vinyl floor covering. We finally found what we believed was a good deal. We agreed on the price and gave the store manager our check.

Not uncommonly, the store subcontracted all of its installation work. Two men came to our home and installed the new kitchen floor right on schedule. There were only two problems:

First, in carrying the vinyl material into the kitchen, they carelessly let it fold over too far and creased it. I'm sure you're aware of what happens when stiff plastic or vinyl is bent and stressed—the color lightens all along the bent area. So, we had a light-colored streak right across the middle of our kitchen floor—an added effect for which we had not bargained.

The second problem was that the workers had failed to remove a small lump of dirt or scrap in one area and when they glued the new floor covering down an unsightly little bump was left in our new floor.

Unfortunately, this story has no happy ending. The installers disappeared, and since the store subcontracted the work, they were able to salve their conscience by saying they were sorry but "it's out of our hands."

Stories like these are all too common and I'm sure you could add several more of your own. In fact, as consumers we have come to expect and accept shoddy service as a fact of life. Because of the emergence of a few service-minded companies, however, such attitudes among consumers are beginning to change.

Businesses on the leading edge of the service issue are finding there are significant benefits to encouraging feedback from customers, especially dissatisfied customers. A Washington, D.C., company called Technical Assistance Research Programs, Inc. (TARP) has conducted studies that reveal much about the importance of providing superior service. For example:

- The average business never hears from 96 percent of its unhappy customers. For every complaint received, the average company in fact has 26 customers with problems, six of which are serious problems.

- Complainers are more likely than non-complainers to do business again with the company that upset them, even if the problem is not satisfactorily resolved.

- Of the customers who register a complaint, between 54 and 70 percent will do business again with the organization if their complaint is resolved. That figure climbs to a staggering 95 percent if the customer feels the complaint was resolved quickly.

- The average customer who has had a problem with an organization tells nine or 10 people about it. Thirteen percent of people who have a problem with an organization recount the incident to more than 20 people.

- Customers who have complained to an organization and had their complaints satisfactorily resolved tell an average of five people about the treatment they received.[1]

TARP also conducted a similar survey specific to banks. Customer retention has gained renewed emphasis in the banking industry and, as a result, many banks are working harder to resolve customer complaints. The study found that resolving complaints to the customer's satisfaction often leads to greater customer loyalty than if the customer never experiences a problem. Findings indicated that 70 to 80 percent of bank customers whose complaints were settled satisfactorily were willing to use additional bank products and services. This compared to only 10 to 20 percent among customers who had not experienced problems.

Specific actions being taken by banks to improve customer satisfaction include:

- A $10 cash payment to any customer finding an error on a checking account statement (National Bank of Detroit).

- Friendly National Bank in Oklahoma City, Oklahoma, regularly surveys new customers to determine how they feel about the service received from bank employees.

- Citibank promptly reimburses customers claiming they were shortchanged by its automatic teller machines—no questions asked.

Obviously, the key to success in handling complaints is not to focus on it as a single transaction. Rather, the complaint should be viewed as one of a series of transactions within a customer relationship that might last for years. The cost of repairing the relationship to the customer's satisfaction must be compared to the revenue the business expects to derive from the average customer. Rarely, if ever, will you find that the cost of resolving a service issue is worth losing a customer.

Summary

No matter what business or occupation you're in, service is an integral part of what you do. Organizations that realize service means "customer focused"—not just at the front line but throughout the entire work force—have a significant strategic advantage. But service doesn't just happen. It is a planned, systematic means of providing for the wants, needs, and desires of your customers.

Studies have indicated that most customers will give you a second chance if you act promptly in correcting a problem. In fact, these individuals might become your most loyal customers. Therefore, you must always weigh the cost of resolving a customer complaint against that of losing a customer.

Reference

1. Albrecht, Karl, and Ronald E. Zemke. *Service America.* Homewood, IL: Dow Jones-Irwin, 1985.

Service As a Marketing Tool

2

The secret to successfully using service as a marketing tool is to build high expectations in the minds of your customers after you have developed a delivery system to consistently meet those expectations.

What business are you in? Do you have competitors who are aggressively going after the same customer as you are? How do you distinguish what you sell from what your competitors have to offer? Do you offer lower cost, higher quality, or better service?

When talking to business owners and managers, it is interesting to note how many of them complain about competitive pressures. For years the response to competition has been to try to undercut them on price or cut them down verbally. But do you know something? Competition is the best thing that can happen to an organization. Approached positively, competition is a powerful motivating force—it sharpens management ability and creativity. It forces us to develop better skills, put more thought into how and why we produce what we sell, clarify our pricing strategies, and, most important of all, it forces us to make a greater effort to understand our customers' wants, needs, desires, and expectations.

Enlightened organizations are beginning to realize that many customers will pay more for a product or service which they perceive as being of higher quality or offering more reliable service. The increasing number of Toyotas, Audis, Saabs, BMWs, Porsches, and Mercedes observed on

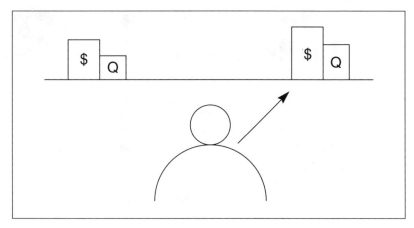

Figure 2.1 Consumers will pay more for perceived quality

U.S. highways is perhaps the most visible support for this statement.

Service can help you distinguish yourself from your competitors and can be used as an extremely valuable marketing tool regardless of what your business is. A dentist in Eugene, Oregon, has recognized the value of perceived service and as a result has done some innovative, thoughtful things for his patients. For example, he gives a fresh, long-stemmed rose to each one of his female patients as she leaves the office. That extra touch goes a long way toward making the experience more memorable in a positive sense. Thus, when one of these patients is asked who her dentist is and if she is satisfied with him, what do you think her response will be? This professional has distinguished himself from his competition for the price of a single rose.

The importance of keeping customers satisfied cannot be overemphasized. As mentioned in Chapter 1, various studies have illustrated that a satisfied buyer tells nine or 10 others about the experience while a significant number of dissatisfied customers will relate their story to more than 20 people. That alone should provide the impetus for us to stop assuming our service is good enough.

When business is going well, we think we're in control and tend to coast. We quote the old maxim, "If it ain't broke, don't fix it." Then when business isn't doing well, we scurry around trying to find ways to reduce costs. Since people represent the largest expense item for most heavily service-oriented businesses, we decide to reduce staff or not to replace anyone who leaves the organization, but what occurs next is even worse. Customer dissatisfaction begins increasing because of a real or perceived decline in service.

A large regional bank offers a good example of the role perception plays in customer satisfaction. After examining teller traffic, management decided to reduce the teller staff by two people, so instead of using seven tellers they had five. This was a good decision based on reliable information, but the plan's execution failed. Customers who had to wait to be helped began to complain that since there were two empty teller windows even at the busiest times, there should be more tellers available. I'm sure you've had similar thoughts when you've been in retail stores where the checkout lines were 10 or 12 people deep and growing, while half a dozen other checkout stands were unattended.

The bank management in the illustration acted quickly and wisely to the negative feedback they were getting from their customers. They physically removed the unused teller stations and the complaints stopped almost immediately, although no other aspect of their service was changed. This is a perfect example of the importance of the customer's perception of your service. What is perceived becomes a reality in the customer's mind.

Paradoxically, there is also a danger in recognizing the importance of service as a marketing tool. There is a strong temptation to over-promise on service delivery capability. Once you have built such high expectations in the minds of your customers, failure to deliver on your promise can be disastrous.

Consider an example from a pizza delivery business. One such company, seeking to capitalize on service, promised, "Served piping hot to your door within 30 minutes or your pizza is free." You can guess what happened. Remember the definition of service: A *system* of providing for the wants, needs, and desires of clients or customers.

Well, this pizza delivery company knew what the customer wanted, but had not developed a reliable system for guaranteeing delivery within 30 minutes. Thus, they ended up delivering a lot of free pizza! Once again the concept was good but its execution was poor. The pizza company has since improved their delivery system but they also modified the promise. Pizzas are no longer free if not delivered within 30 minutes, instead a discount is given. How much better it would have been had they thought their service strategy through more carefully and made the modified offer in the beginning.

When someone mentions the word marketing, most people immediately conjure up an image of an elaborate advertising campaign that costs a lot of money. Many business people, however, have found that some of their most effective marketing efforts cost them little or nothing.

There is a service station in my neighborhood that has built an excellent business and a loyal clientele while spending virtually nothing on conventional advertising, and their gasoline prices are among the highest in town. Do you know how they do it? Their success is due primarily to three things:

First, they make every attempt to call you by name even if they have to read it from your check or credit card. They know that people generally like to be addressed by name.

Secondly, they don't over-promise. They only do the work that has been requested unless they have contacted the customer and secured permission to do something further. Customers never feel pressured and they guarantee their work for a reasonable period.

Finally, when the customer comes to pick up the car, they take the time to explain what was done and why. Time spent educating your customers is time well-spent. Such personal concern and attention goes a long way toward building a lasting and profitable business relationship. Do you know how this service station gets new customers? You guessed it—referrals by the dozens.

The customer first, last, and always. This slogan is emblazoned on the hearts and minds of every employee in organizations committed to separating themselves from their competitors based on service. A good friend of mine operates a successful space planning, interior design, and architectural firm which is based solidly on doing what is best for the client, regardless of the consequences to the project's profitability. The need for complete openness and honesty with clients and coworkers is drilled into every employee.

If he or one of his people makes a mistake on one of their projects, he will absorb the cost of correcting it rather than trying to slide it by the client or make excuses. That company also has worked on projects where something has gone wrong because of circumstances beyond their control, but they are being blamed for the failure by the client. In such situations the owner often covers the expense of fixing the problem because he knows the value of a satisfied customer and the impact such a customer can have on future business. This philosophy has served him well through the years. Goodwill multiplies its value, but ill will expands exponentially.

To this point we've discussed the importance of customer perception, expectations, and satisfaction, but the question remains, "How do you get inside your customers' minds to find out what they like and dislike so you know whether your marketing and service efforts are on target?" There's only one way, and that is to ask them.

Probably one of the best examples of an organization that constantly requests its customers' opinions is Stew Leonard's Company. That firm is an extraordinary dairy store featured in a 1985 PBS film by Sam Taylor and John Nathan titled "In Search of Excellence." In addition to providing a suggestion box for customer comments, Stew Leonard regularly calls in groups of customers for focus group meetings. The intent of these meetings is to provide a setting in which there is an open and honest exchange between the store's management and its customers regarding the store in general, new ideas management is considering, and the opinions and attitudes of the customers toward certain aspects of the store.

At one of these meetings a lady stood up and said, "I don't like your fish." When asked to explain why she didn't like the fish she said, "It's not fresh. I like to go to a fish market and buy fresh fish."

The manager in charge of the fish section was also at the meeting and said, "What do you mean it's not fresh? We get it fresh from Boston piers every morning. I guarantee you it's fresh."

To that the lady replied, "But it's packaged in a [plastic-wrapped] supermarket package."

So the store management decided to immediately set up a fresh fish bar with ice in it. Now they offer wrapped fish in one section and, across the aisle, the fresh fish bar where people can buy it right off the ice at the same price.

After the change was made, store owner Stew Leonard said, "Our packaged fish sales didn't decrease at all, but we doubled our total fish sales. We were doing about 15,000 pounds a week; now we're doing 30,000 pounds a week."

Not a bad payback for taking time to listen to a customer, is it?

Summary

Contrary to what many of us might prefer to think, competition is good for any organization. It keeps us on our toes and goads us into finding better ways to serve our customers. The good news is that customers will pay more for a product or service they perceive as being of higher quality or offering greater reliability.

Service is an excellent way to distinguish your organization from your competitors, and the number of possible ways to enhance what you do is limited only by your imagination (remember the dentist who gives a fresh rose to each of his female patients). But don't promise more than you can deliver. The secret to successfully using service as a marketing tool is to build high expectations in your customers' minds *after* you have developed a delivery system that allows you to consistently meet those expectations.

Defining Service for Your Organization

3

Assumption is the lowest form of knowledge. Service can be defined only from the customer's perspective.

A good friend of mine is fond of saying, "Assumption is the lowest form of knowledge." I repeat that statement every chance I get because it's so true, especially when it involves understanding customer needs, wants, and expectations.

Organizations often go to great lengths to provide a product or service they assume customers want. An excellent example can be found in the credit card industry. In the early 1980s, one of the country's largest credit card issuers decided to offer a "premiere" card. The premiere card was designed to appeal to the more affluent members of our society—the *upscale customer,* in banking jargon. It carried a larger credit line, offered free credit card protection service (in the event the card is lost or stolen), and provided for the purchase of name brand merchandise at discounted prices along with several other optional privileges and services. The annual membership fee for the premiere card was double that of the regular card.

Somewhere in this new card's development and its accompanying services, it was decided that the availability of a toll-free, 24-hour customer service telephone number would be crucial to the card's success. The rest of the development group agreed and the cardholder services operations managers were asked to organize equipment and staff adequate to handle 24-hour service. Having someone available to answer telephone calls 24 hours a day, however, is expensive.

Approximately two years after the premiere card's introduction, a customer research study was conducted. It was designed to determine customer expectations and satisfaction on key service elements. One of the questions asked customers what hours of the day and days of the week they would like to be able to call the cardholder services center with inquiries regarding their card. Guess what the response was? Only a small minority felt 24-hour service was necessary. Although management might have decided to go ahead and offer such service regardless of customer preference, it would have been helpful to have had access to this information during the initial decision-making process.

Service can be defined only from the customer's perspective. Before any organization can truly define service, it must have input from its present and potential customers. Assuming you know what people want can result in customer dissatisfaction or even financial disaster. The world of business is littered with organizations founded on good products which filled a definite need but failed to gain customer support because of what customers perceived as inferior or poor service.

So much valuable information can be gained by asking customers a few simple questions.

Let's examine the banking industry in more detail. In many cases they've given the public good reason to pick on them. At present, most banks have branch offices at various locations within a city and throughout a certain geographical region. Now, considering all the talk about service as a key strategic element in gaining a competitive advantage, what is the most common complaint you've heard about service in banking? Usually the complaint is, "They're always moving people around. They have these people called 'personal bankers' but I never know who will be there to help me when I stop in. When I ask about the previous person, I always get the same answer, 'He/she was trans-ferred to another department or branch.' How can they get to know me and I them if they keep shuffling people around all the time? I liked it better the way it used to be when I had someone who I really felt was *my* banker." Does that com-plaint sound familiar? You've probably said the same thing.

The typical response from the bank's management is that, "We're making the best use of our human resources and providing advancement opportunities for them." In some cases this might be true, but in others, staff members are simply moved as a matter of expedience without con-sideration to customer impact.

So, what do your customers think about the service being provided by your organization? How do your custom-ers define good service? The answer to these questions can be determined through market research. Now, don't get excited. Market research need not be complex or expensive in order to provide you with useful information on customer attitudes and opinions—and you don't have to be a statis-tical expert.

Richard Thalheimer is owner and president of The Sharper Image, a successful San Francisco-based company that sells mostly high-tech products through direct mail catalogs and retail stores. He says ad hoc interviews with ordinary people can tell you more about what your custom-ers want than a stack of market research studies. In an interview printed in the July 1986, issue of "Working Smart," a monthly newsletter, he relates that as a catalog was coming off the press, several of his people didn't think the photo on it's cover looked right.

When his production manager called him from Atlanta to tell him about the problem, Thalheimer instructed him to grab a few copies and take the next flight to San Francisco. Thalheimer met the production manager at the airport and then decided to do a little market testing of his own. He showed copies of the catalog to the first 10 people who came by and asked them what they thought of the cover. Most of them said they thought it was great. He decided then and there to go ahead with the cover, and it turned out to be one of the company's most successful catalogs.

Thalheimer said the experience taught him that, "You don't have to spend a fortune to find out what people like. A sample of 10 can be pretty reliable." The experts would argue the validity of such an approach, but what else would you expect from those who make their living complicating things for you?

Market research simply means asking people to share their honest thoughts with you. You may be asking them for information related to specific issues or just providing an opportunity for them to air their feelings on any topic relating to your organization. Usually you will want a combination of both. Regardless of the method you use to gather information, it is important to collect and record your findings in an organized manner so they can be analyzed and used to make better, more profitable decisions.

One of the most inexpensive ways to obtain customer feedback is to provide a suggestion box that is placed in a convenient and non-intimidating area of your store. Don't place it next to the manager's office or the checkout counter.

Stew Leonard's dairy store (discussed in Chapter 2) has used the suggestion box idea with overwhelming success. For example, one customer suggested that it would be nice if strawberries were set out in bulk so customers could select the berries and exact quantities they wanted rather than selling them prepackaged in cartons. The store tried the idea and strawberry sales increased dramatically because the average customer bagged more berries than the previously used containers held.

Employees should also not be overlooked as a valuable source of suggestions for improving customer service. After all employees, not managers, are the people who have the most direct contact with customers. Employees' ideas often not only improve service, but result in cost savings to the company. Many companies have implemented formal employee suggestion programs. Some pay cash awards equivalent to a percentage of the annual savings resulting from the employee's suggestion. Patrick L. Townsend illustrates this point by telling about the suggestion program that existed at The Paul Revere Insurance Companies before they moved to a quality team approach. In its last year, their program yielded 216 suggestions. Eighty-six of those suggestions were implemented and resulted in savings of $41,000.[1] So, not only did the company improve its operations, it also saved a significant amount of money.

Simple surveys also provide an effective means of obtaining customer feedback on specific issues. In using either phone or mail surveys, the most critical element is the questionnaire. It is important to think through exactly what the purpose of the survey is and to word the questions in such a way as to make them as objective and unbiased as possible.

For example, if you are interested in finding out how customers feel about having to wait in line at the checkout counter, you shouldn't ask, "Do you mind having to wait in line at the checkout counter?" The wording of that question begs a negative response. It would be better to pose the question so that a rated response can be given.

Example
Waiting in line two minutes or less at the checkout counter is (circle one)

Quite acceptable	Somewhat acceptable	Neither acceptable nor unacceptable	Somewhat unacceptable	Quite unacceptable
1	2	3	4	5

or

I don't mind waiting in line at the checkout stand if the wait is no longer than (check one)

____ 1 minute ____ 2 minutes ____ 3 minutes ____ 4 minutes
____ It is never acceptable to have to wait.

If you're planning a direct mail survey, it's best to limit the questionnaire to no more than two pages—one page is best. A telephone survey with the customer should take no more than 10 to 15 minutes to complete.

A question that always arises when the subject of research studies is being discussed is, "How many people should we survey to ensure our information is valid?" The answer to that question depends on what type of study you're conducting. If you are interested in asking a number of customers for ideas and comments on a specific service, approximately 30 responses are needed. After 30 responses, repetition of the major thoughts increases rapidly and little new information is gained by surveying more people.

If you are conducting a survey in a limited geographical area using a standard questionnaire, 100 to 200 responses will yield the group's general attitudes. On the other hand, a regional study covering several cities or a few states normally requires 300 to 400 responses to obtain a fairly reliable response. A sample of 1,200 to 1,500 people generally reflects the opinions and feelings of the national population on most subjects.

These sample sizes are based on general rules of thumb and are estimates, but they have proven to give reliable data in all but unusual situations. For the purpose of determining customer attitudes and opinions the suggested sample sizes should be adequate. Just don't get hung up on being overly precise or you'll find the samples and expenses will have to be much larger.

Another option in getting information from your customers is formation of a focus group. Focus groups frequently are used to acquire customer feedback on a wide variety of topics and issues in a fairly short time frame. In these instances, groups of customers (usually eight to 12) are asked to participate in a round table discussion of their likes and dislikes and their thoughts regarding various ideas being considered by management. Often participants are given an incentive of nominal value in appreciation for donating their time. If you are just starting to use focus groups, it may be wise to hire a professional facilitator to lead the discussions for the first sessions.

Now that we have a general idea of the mechanics of gathering customer feedback concerning service, what questions should we ask them? It is helpful to think of service as having four major components: convenience, accuracy, responsiveness, and timeliness.

Convenience simply means that we have designed our service delivery system so that it is as simple to access and use as possible from the customer's perspective. *Accuracy* implies that we do it right the first time every time—with no mistakes that are perceptible to the customer. Being ready to react as quickly as possible to a customer's needs is what *responsiveness* entails. Often this requires flexibility and resourcefulness on the part of our customer contact people. Finally, *timeliness* refers to the length of time it requires for us to meet the customer's needs. This could involve the length of time required to process an insurance claim, the number of times the phone rings before we answer the customer's call, or the time required to build a customer's garage.

The customer has built-in expectations regarding each of the four components of service. These expectations have been acquired over a period of time based on previous experiences, advertising claims, and comments from friends and relatives. It is the job of every organization to understand the expectations of its customers in terms of convenience, accuracy, responsiveness, and timeliness. Once those expectations are understood, the company's managers must build service delivery systems that meet or surpass them.

Therefore, the questions asked of customers should be based on these four service components. Examples include:

- How satisfied are you with how quickly we answer the phone?

- Have we made an error on your account within the last three months? If so, what was the error?

- How quickly did we resolve the problem?

- How satisfied were you with the length of time required to resolve the problem?

- How would you rate the courtesy of our employees?

- How would you rate the professionalism of our employees?

- How would you rate our employees' ability to help you?

- After we finished the remodeling of your building, how satisfied were you with our cleanup job?

- How satisfied were you with the length of time it took to return our bid to you?

- How satisfied were you with the length of time required to process your application?

As you can see, the number of questions that can be developed is almost unlimited. So, try to focus on those questions you feel are most critical to helping you run your organization—those that relate to things you can control. Always provide an opportunity for the customer to add something that you may not have considered by allowing adequate space at the end of the survey for comments or suggestions.

Summary

Assumption is the lowest form of knowledge. Never assume you know what the customer wants, especially when you're considering service. Service only can be defined from the customer's perspective and you can find out what customers think only by asking them.

Customer feedback can be obtained in many ways, several of which are fairly simple and inexpensive. Alternative research methods include: focus groups, telephone surveys, mail surveys, suggestion boxes for customers, and suggestion programs for employees. Customer-contact employees often are an overlooked source of valuable information about customer wants and needs.

If you plan to stay in business, you must find a way of learning what your customers think of your organization's performance.

Reference

1. Townsend, Patrick L. *Commit to Quality.* New York: John Wiley & Sons, Inc., 1986.

Measuring Service Performance

4

There is no way to know if you are winning the service game without a scorecard.

If you are serious about improving the level of service provided by your business, you must develop a means of objectively measuring performance. The question then becomes, "What do we measure?"

First of all, the measurement of service performance should be divided into two categories: internal and external measures. *Internal measures* track the performance of employees and processes within the organization, including error and productivity rates. *External measures* are those service components that are perceptible to the customer, including accuracy and turnaround time. Obviously, the internal measures are directly related to the external measures, and in reality they basically track the same things but from different perspectives—what is good from the organization's point of view and what is satisfactory to the customer.

It is impossible to develop a comprehensive set of specific measures appropriate to all types of businesses in one chapter. There are, however, certain basic measurements that are applicable to virtually every operating unit within any organization. One measurement is the volume of work passing through the unit in terms of input and output. For example, assume you are responsible for supervising a group of customer service representatives handling mail and phone inquiries as well as walk-in traffic. Each representative should keep a log sheet on which he/she records the number of phone calls, mail pieces, and walk-ins handled each day. From these log sheets, totals for the entire unit can be tabulated.

Now, consideration of work volumes alone won't provide enough information. Accuracy of the work, productivity, unit cost, timeliness, and backlogs also should be tracked to provide a more complete picture of an operating unit's overall performance.

Unless your organization is large enough to have its own quality assurance unit, the most common method of measuring accuracy of work done by a unit is for the supervisor to randomly select and check completed items each day. Although there are established formulas for determining how many items (sample size) should be reviewed based on the total number of items processed, a general rule of thumb is that you should check approximately 30 items per month per employee. Supervisors should examine the accuracy of individual employees and the unit as a whole.

Tracking productivity requires that you know the volume of work processed and the actual number of paid hours expended in performing the work. The formula for calculating the productivity rate is simple—divide the volume completed by the paid hours required. Once again, accurate record keeping is critical to the integrity of the results. Using our previous example of a customer service group, this means each representative must record productive time separately from idle time or time spent on miscellaneous activities. Again, productivity should be tracked at both the individual and unit levels in order that month-to-month and employee-to-employee comparisons can be made.

Unit costs are an excellent means of evaluating manager performance, but they are used rather infrequently in organizations that provide a service as opposed to a manufactured product. The primary reason unit cost is so seldom tracked is because of a natural tendency to make the calculation so complex that it becomes too cumbersome to be practical to use on an ongoing basis. The good news is that there is a simple method available that has proven its usefulness time and again. The formula is:

$$\text{Unit Cost} = \frac{\text{Hours required} \times \text{Average hourly salary}}{\text{Volume of work completed}}$$

(Average hourly salary includes the cost of fringe benefits.)

The concept of unit cost is particularly valuable when you have two or more units performing similar functions at the same or different locations. Differences in staffing, experience, and other efficiencies appear quickly under the light of unit cost.

Timeliness refers to the length of time required to process an item or perform a job from start to finish. Both the customer and the organization are concerned about timeliness when dealing with the time required to pack and ship an order. On the other hand, it is the business that is concerned with how quickly customer payments are processed. A business wants its receipts credited to its account as quickly as possible.

Backlogs refer to the inventory or work-in-progress already in-house and waiting to be processed. Effective management of backlogs is critical to keeping customer dissatisfaction due to timeliness problems to a minimum.

The particular business you are in will determine the specific performance measurements you will want to have in place. Such measures should be developed on a unit-by-unit basis to ensure no critical measurements are missed.

Each operating unit should be required to submit at least a weekly performance report to senior management. Allowing reports to be turned in any less frequently than once per week introduces the risk of failing to identify problems before significant damage has been done. An example of a simple report for an order entry unit is shown in Figure 4.1. If this information is kept over a long period of time, it can be useful in forecasting future volumes and identifying trends in backlogs, productivity, accuracy, timeliness, and unit cost. You will then be in an enviable position compared to competitors who do not have similar information available to them.

Management Information Report for Order Entry Unit

Today's date _____

	Today	Month to date	Forecast	Over/ (Under) forecast
Beginning holdover	_____			
New orders rec'd	_____	_____	_____	_____
Orders processed	_____	_____		
Ending holdover	_____			
Regular paid hours	_____	_____		
Overtime hours	_____	_____		
Total paid hours	_____	_____		

		Goal	Over/ (under) goal
Productivity rate*	_____	_____	_____	_____
Unit cost**		_____	_____	_____
Accuracy	_____	_____	_____	_____
System downtime/problems:	_____		

Absences: _____

Other issues: _____

*Productivity rate equals Orders processed divided by Total paid hours.
**Unit cost equals Cost of total paid hours (regular time including benefits plus overtime) divided by Orders processed.

Figure 4.1 Example of a simple report for order entry unit

Graphing order entry information will provide you with some major insights into the workings of your operations. The type of information I suggest you collect and report can be developed for virtually any organizational function. Prime targets for implementation in service areas include high-volume, paper-intensive, or transaction-oriented functions such as:

Data entry	Accounts payable
Payment processing	Clerical support groups
Word processing	Mail-room operations
Claim processing	Microfilm processing
Application processing	Customer service units
Statement processing	Telemarketing

By no means should the above be considered an exhaustive list. Applications exist in almost any organization, no matter how large or small.

As was previously stated, some external measures are no different from internal measures, but in the case of external measures, we are asking the customer to evaluate our performance on key aspects of our service. Typically, this is done by surveying customers on a regular basis.

If you've recently purchased a new automobile, you have probably received a survey form from the manufacturer asking you to rate your satisfaction with such things as:

- Body construction.

- Electrical/mechanical systems.

- Paint finish.

- Ride and handling.

- Salesperson's knowledge of the product.

- Professionalism of the salesperson.

- Repair service required, if any.

There are numerous other items manufacturers have found of value in analyzing consumer satisfaction and possible ways to improve their products.

Hotels and restaurants often use postcard-size comment cards to obtain regular feedback from their customers. Bill Marriott, founder of the Marriott Hotel chain, read every single comment card for over 50 years and attributed much of his company's success to understanding and responding to the customer. Reread that last sentence. There's an important point there that I don't want you to miss. Marriott talked not only about understanding the customer but also about *responding* to that customer. Knowledge without action is of no value to anyone. (For more information on the how to of conducting customer surveys see Chapter 3.)

As you evaluate your service, don't overlook the possibility of shopping your competitors. This is a common method of finding new ideas and staying current with what the competition is doing, especially among restaurants and retailers. Usually business people are familiar with their local competition and if they aren't, they should be. Some of the best ideas, however, come from visiting stores in other cities around the country as you travel. Encourage your employees to visit these stores, too.

If you run a customer service operation, try calling the customer service center of a major competitor to see how quickly they pick up the phone and how well they handle your inquiry. Learn all you can about what your competition is doing.

Summary

You will never know if you're winning the service game without a scorecard. You need a reliable means of measuring performance all the way down to the individual employee level. Measuring performance is not as difficult as it might appear.

There should be key measures for both internal and external performance indicators. Internal measurements focus on the organizational view of how you're doing. External measurements gauge customer perceptions through surveys and shopping the competition.

At a minimum, internal measures should include volume, accuracy, productivity, timeliness, backlogs, and unit cost. External measures are gathered by surveying customers. Those surveys provide insight for the level of satisfaction that can be attributed to the various components of a product, service, or both.

Remember, understanding the customer is not enough. Once you understand the customer's attitudes and opinions, you must take action in response to your findings. Knowledge without action is of no value to anyone.

What Not to Do

5

Don't fall victim to the "We are so powerful we can do anything" syndrome.

Experience is a great teacher, but to spare ourselves some grief and heartache we should learn everything we can from the experience of others. In previous chapters we've already touched on some of the don'ts, but they warrant repeating in a chapter all their own. The following examples are not an exhaustive list of things to avoid, but they are the problems that seem to appear with the most frequency among organizations attempting to improve their customer service.

• Don't move too quickly.

The habit of constantly trying to implement new ideas results in a helter-skelter approach to improvement. Consideration should be given to how an idea fits in with your long-range objectives and the potential impact it will have on employees, suppliers, subcontractors, and middle managers. A planned method of evaluating the idea's contribution to the organization also should be developed before implementation. Too many changes taking place simultaneously make it almost impossible to determine how successful any one idea is.

If you run a bookstore, don't rearrange the books, lower the checkout platform, enlarge the magazine selection, change the window display, and make staffing changes all at once. Rather, experiment with each of these alterations one at a time so you can note effect(s) of each action.

- Don't fail to communicate the what, how, and why of your service improvement efforts before you start to take action.

Despite the fact that you're the boss, your employees are the ones who must attempt to make your ideas work. Tell them what you're thinking about and request their input. You might be surprised at the things they know about the service process that you don't.

Don't make the same mistake as the company that spent over $100,000 on a special three-hour event for its board of directors. At the conclusion of that expensive production, the company asked its managers to make staff cuts so they could come in on budget for the year. The long-term damage caused by the message such an action sends is immeasurable.

- Don't become so preoccupied with the improvement system that you lose sight of your real objectives.

Too often, the system itself becomes all-consuming. There is a feeling that the system must be technically perfect in every aspect in order to be credible to all the stakeholders within the organization. The result is an exercise in political gamesmanship and creative number-crunching designed to support the desired outcome. What is actually happening is hidden beneath mountains of fabricated and/or extraneous data, but management can claim it has done an excellent job of addressing service issues because they have an impressive report that shows all is well.

• Don't become obsessed with numbers and constant tightening of service standards.

Do what is logical and rational—the things that really make sense in light of what you know about your customers, your employees, and your organization's key long-range objective. I have witnessed situations where top-level executives ordered service standards to be tightened beyond what is reasonable, considering the factors involved. Then they demanded that operations managers "meet the numbers," or else. The standards were met—on paper. In reality, the operating managers changed the ground rules in the operations areas so that some of what was previously unacceptable became acceptable in order to meet the goal. Yet, those involved adamantly denied that this occurred. Their obsession with numbers had created a fairytale kingdom where it was difficult to distinguish between fantasy and reality.

That example is a perfect lead-in to the next point.

• Don't use threats, intimidation, and scare tactics to force service improvement.

Admittedly the short-term results from such an approach can yield positive change for the organization as a whole, but in the long run, the result is high turnover, low morale, and forced creativity in reporting of performance data. Worst of all, such abuse of power damages the self-esteem of the employees and makes it difficult for them to take pride in their work. They know what should be done but they are pressured into taking shortcuts in order to make the numbers. Things are no longer black or white—a gray fog sets in that covers a multitude of sins. The integrity of the employees is slowly eroded along with that of the organization, but employees are locked in; they are afraid to rock the boat. If they do question what is going on, they fear they might lose their jobs and they can't afford that.

Too many managers are too far removed from their people to realize or care about the precarious situation in which they have placed their employees. The non-verbal message to employees is that, "Honesty is *not* the best policy." It's OK to bend the rules if it makes the organization look better.

- Don't assume service will improve simply because you've mandated it, and you're the boss.

Unless you are willing to personally demonstrate commitment to improving service, you will not be taken seriously. Employees will do just enough to get by, because they've seen these fads come and go many times before. A corollary to this point is:

- Don't count on slogans, buttons, balloons, and free lunches to solve your service problems and maintain morale.

Words without actions are devoid of meaning and you might as well be speaking into a black hole. Today's employees can quickly distinguish between sincerity and mere lip service.

- Don't fail to share your service philosophy with all your employees from janitor to chairman of the board.

If everyone feels he/she has a part in the process, no matter how small, a positive service attitude will soon permeate the organization. A phenomenon known as synergism occurs whereby the combined actions of all involved have a greater effect than the sum of the actions of the individuals involved.

- Don't assume that middle managers will automatically buy into the proposed improvement process.

Usually such improvement efforts have the greatest impact on middle managers. Often they must work harder, at least initially, and have to change their standard methods of operation. Such changes are not met with shouts of joy and enthusiasm. If you fail to win them over, they can quickly sabotage your best-laid plans. Again, your willingness to demonstrate your personal commitment to the process is critical in welding your people into a unified force ready to march into the service battle.

- Don't even think about beginning a service improvement effort, if you aren't sure you are willing to allocate the required resources to it, "come hell or high water."

To make a significant start and then back off, even for a short period, raises serious questions in the minds of your people. They begin to doubt your sincerity, and see it as a halfhearted attempt not worthy of their concern and commitment.

- Don't let short-term goals interfere with the improvement process.

One company suspended its quality assurance function for the entire month of December in order to meet their headcount numbers. All overtime was eliminated and temporary employees were laid off for the month. Those employees were replaced by quality assurance staff members, thus total headcount was lowered enough to meet the predetermined goal. In reality, the company was understaffed during this period, and customer service deteriorated as a result. Such action demonstrates shortsightedness and improper priorities on management's part.

- Don't assume your people know how to provide good service.

Evaluate your current training program. Key elements that should be covered are product knowledge, communication skills, and any required machine/technical skills. The staff should also have at least a general knowledge of what other departments within the organization do. Give them information about your customers and competitors. The more knowledge you can give them the better. Consider refresher courses. No one can be trained once and for all.

- Don't assume the tools, equipment, and procedures you have in place are adequate.

Encourage feedback on these issues from your employees. A major company had several temporary employees opening mail with table knives borrowed from the cafeteria. It doesn't take a genius to see that there must be a better way of opening mail. Countless examples like this can be found in companies throughout the United States. That's one of the reasons Tom Peters (co-author of *In Search of Excellence*) and others encourage Management By Walking Around (MBWA). You won't be able to cause any kind of improvement if you don't know what's going on in the trenches.

- Don't fall victim to the "We are so powerful we can do anything" syndrome.

A 1987 article in *The Wall Street Journal* compared the arrogance, abuse of power, desire for wealth, and lack of respect for others demonstrated by many of today's leaders to the tragic Greek and Shakespearean characters in classic literature.

For example, Ajax is considered "top gun" among the Greeks in the Trojan War. In battle, he is likened to a lion, and enemy soldiers are understandably awed. Sophocles reveals Ajax's tragic flaw when Ajax is denied a promotion. The affront so rankles him that he seeks revenge by murdering the Greek leaders, but the gods intervene and turn him on the Greeks' livestock. After coming to his senses the next day, he is so overcome with shame that he kills himself.

Ajax's crime is not that he slaughtered a few goats and sheep, or attempted revenge on his unappreciative bosses. His real offense is arrogance.

Early in the play the youthful Ajax, leaving home to join the Greek army, is offered some parting advice by his father: "My son, seek victory in arms, but seek it always with the help of heaven."

Ajax blusters, "Father, with the help of the gods even a weak man might win, but I, even without their aid, trust to bring glory within my group."

Such characters inevitably came to a swift and unenviable end. In the words of the Greek historian Therodotus, "The gods are accustomed to throw down whatever rises too high."[1]

Summary

Service improvement, like any major organizational initiative, is fraught with pitfalls to avoid. The underlying message of this chapter is that respect for the individual; good, two-way communication; and a well-thought-out plan based on facts rather than assumptions (all mixed with a little humility) are the keys to implementing a successful service improvement process within an organization. You can't do it alone. You and your employees must do it together.

Reference

1. Clemons, John K. "Wall Street and the Age-Old Tragic Flaw, " *The Wall Street Journal,* March 18, 1987: 30.

The Five Principles of Service

6

If you take care of your people and your customers, they will take care of you.

No one can claim that there are *only* five principles of service, but there are at least five that are crucial for achieving a superior level of service. They provide an excellent foundation for building a successful business enterprise.

1. Pay attention to the little things.

2. Do business by the golden rule.

3. Understand the customer.

4. Encourage innovation.

5. Value your people.

As you begin to contemplate service as it relates to your organization and how to apply the five principles listed, it's important to remember the definition of service given in Chapter 3. Service is a *system* of satisfactorily providing for the wants, needs, and desires of clients or customers. It's an orderly set of guidelines, policies, and criteria that has been established and communicated to all employees in order to satisfy the customer. In other words, certain requirements must be met in order for the transaction to be considered successful by both parties.

Unfortunately, such a well-defined service system does not exist in many companies. We simply assume that employees know what constitutes good service. Therefore, the first thing we must do is define what good service looks like and communicate that vision to all employees. Further, this service vision must be made specific to each employee's job functions so they have a means of determining if their work is conforming to requirements.

• Principle No. 1–Paying attention to the little things.

Let's consider answering customer phone calls. What is the requirement going to be? How should customer service representatives greet the caller? Is a simple "Hello" sufficient or do we want more? It might be that our definition of service suggests it is more appropriate to say "Good afternoon. Acme Business Services, Mr. Beech speaking, how can I help you?" The addition of these simple details to the call opening makes a faceless transaction more personal and memorable. Of course, you have to handle the rest of the transaction correctly, too, or your added efforts have gone for naught.

If your only contact with a customer is by phone, the manner in which you answer the phone can have a significant impact on their perception of your company. The employees who are answering your phone or making outgoing calls to customers should realize that, to the customer, *they are the company!*

One organization that recognized the importance of handling phone calls in a professional manner tried an interesting experiment. They placed eye-level mirrors at each telephone representative's desk. On the bottom of the mirror these words were printed, "How would you feel if you were talking to a person who looked like this?" The effect was significant and positive. Since these people were on the phone constantly, seeing themselves in the questioning mirror helped to break the monotony of their day. It tempted them to smile and added enthusiasm to the tone of their voice.

Let's examine another example of attention to detail that wins customer loyalty. I recently went to a local pharmacy which I had not patronized previously to have a medical prescription filled. After a courteous greeting, the pharmacist put the prescribed capsules in a container, dropped them in a bag and said the total was $8.90. I handed him a personal check in payment. He looked at it and said, "Thank you, Mr. Butterfield." To me, the sound of that phrase had a nice ring to it.

Our names are important identifiers of our individuality and most of us like to be called by name even if we know the one talking to us picked it up from our check or credit card. In this case, not only did the pharmacist call me by name, he also took the time to explain in layman's terms what the medicine was supposed to do and the appropriate dosage, even though the required information was on the label. He personalized what otherwise would have been a sterile transaction. He distinguished himself from other pharmacists in my mind, and the fact that I've repeated this story several times to friends and acquaintances hasn't hurt his business any either.

John Naisbitt in his book *Megatrends*,[1] refers to this principle as high-tech/high-touch. We are living in a world that is becoming increasingly automated and technically oriented, yet people are hungry for more personal contact and interaction. They don't want to be treated as just another number.

Pay attention to the little things. What can you do in your own situation? If customers come to your desk, do you keep it neat? If you have ashtrays setting around, do you keep them clean? Are documents you've prepared for customers neat, clean, and uniform in appearance? Do you do a good job of cleaning up after you've finished a remodeling job? Are the chairs in your waiting area comfortable?

Smile and remember to say thank-you.

• Principle No. 2–Doing business by the golden rule.

Essentially, doing business by the golden rule means that if you take care of your people and your customers, they will take care of you. We need to assume the servant's role of supporting, assisting, and providing for our people and our customers. If seeing yourself in the role of a servant rubs you the wrong way, you might have some attitude adjusting to do, but, I'd venture to say you're not alone.

Many of us would rather see ourselves in the role of the master, wouldn't we? The desire for power, prestige, money, and empire-building often obstructs our ability to do business by the golden rule. (For some individuals, reading this paragraph will result in immediate rationalization, denial, and finger-pointing.)

To determine where you stand on this principle, give yourself the following test based on an illustration often used by Tom Peters. Imagine you work in a retail store where you have just finished giving the place a thorough cleaning, arranged the displays, stocked the shelves, and made sure that everything is neat and tidy. You go to unlock the door and you see the clearance sale crowd is already there pressing to get in. What's your first reaction? Is it, "Oh no! Here come the animals"? Or is it the Disney philosophy of, "Great. Our guests are here"? The answer that most closely approximates your initial response to the situation described, will give you a good idea of how well you practice the golden rule principle.

One way to foster positive feelings about the customer is by compiling and circulating compliments and complimentary letters received from customers. Post the latest ones on a bulletin board for all to see. Too often, our entire focus is on the complaints registered by customers, and the good news is ignored and forgotten.

As for your people, sincere recognition for a job well done and constructive feedback on their progress are the most effective means of building a competent and loyal work force. High-tech/high-touch applies just as much to your employees as it does to your customers. Figure 6.1 graphically portrays the importance of maintaining positive morale.

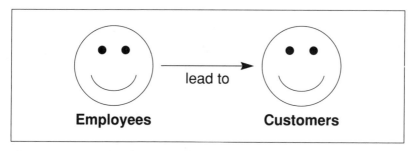

Figure 6.1 Importance of a positive morale

My opinion is that informal recognition and feedback provide 80 percent of the external motivation for employees to do a good job, while the remaining 20 percent comes from formal efforts such as employee of the month awards, etc. So don't underestimate the value of personal involvement and interaction with your people.

Do business by the golden rule. See yourself as serving your customer and employees. Why? It seems to have something to do with the old saying, "You reap what you sow." Why is it we always must be reminded of that?

• Principle No. 3–Understanding the customer.

When it comes to understanding the customer, many of us get caught in the trap of making assumptions without getting cold, hard facts. To understand the customer, we need an effective means of getting feedback from them. In one of my "previous lives," I worked for a company that realized the importance of such feedback. We developed a one-page questionnaire that was sent to over 1,000 customers each month to discover how they felt about specific issues and to request their comments. In addition, we hired consultants to conduct research on special service issues.

You'll be surprised at what you can find out from these efforts. One company learned that, in general, their customers prefer to be transferred to another person after they have given their reason for calling because they then feel they are dealing with an expert. The company's assumption had been that people didn't like to be transferred, period.

Understand your customers. Without customers you're out of business. (For more on understanding the customer, see Chapter 3.)

- Principle No. 4—Encourage innovation.

The people who know the most about any business are the front-line people. In the banking business, the tellers, customer service, and other customer-contact people can tell you whether money is coming in or going out, whether the public is optimistic or pessimistic, and who's offering the greatest competition. These employees are an excellent barometer for whether or not a new product or service is going to be successful—they know the customer. They know what works and what doesn't because they *do* the work. Those who are managers just think about doing work. (W. Edwards Deming, often called the father of quality control, says, "American management on the whole has a negative scrap value. It's like an old refrigerator you can't sell. You have to pay someone $25 to cart it off."[2])

The best ideas for improving products, services, or service delivery systems come from the people who actually do the work. *Encourage innovation.* Ask employees for their thoughts and impressions. And do not forget to sincerely recognize their contributions!

- Principle No. 5—Value your people.

This is perhaps the most important principle of all, for if your people don't feel they are a valued part of the organization, they will have difficulty valuing the customer and providing quality service.

Begin by telling them exactly what you expect of them. They can't win the game if they don't know the rules. Let them know how their performance will be evaluated. If performance is based on productivity, attendance, and accuracy, tell them and explain precisely how each of these three factors is measured. Don't introduce surprises when review time rolls around.

Second, listen to them. Get out on the floor and find out what their problems and concerns are. Do they have the training and equipment they need to meet your standards of performance? Give them ongoing feedback on how they're doing. Don't just pat them on the back once a year and say, "Good job," whether they need it or not. They must know the score before the end of the game.

Finally, catch them doing something *right* and reward them for it. The reward can take many forms, but don't overlook the value of a sincere thank-you for a job well done *in front of their peers.*

Value your people so that when a crunch comes, and crunches inevitably do, your people will bust their buns for you. Your boss will think you're great, to say nothing of the tremendous comfort that comes from knowing your people are for you, not against you.

Summary

Many years ago, a man by the name of William Danforth, founder of the Ralston Purina Company, wrote a little book entitled *I Dare You* in which he dares his readers to be the best they can be. He dares them to succeed. In this chapter, we've discussed the five principles of service. These principles are not automatic. You cannot implement them by simple edict. There is no magic formula, it must start with you and me. So, I dare you to:

1. Pay attention to the little things.

2. Do business by the golden rule.

3. Understand the customer.

4. Encourage innovation.

5. Value your people.

References

1. Naisbitt, John. *Megatrends*. New York: Warner Books, 1982.

2. Main, Jeremy. "The Old Curmudgeon Who Talks Tough on Quality." *Fortune* 105, No. 12 (June 25, 1984): 118–122.

Communicating with the Customer

7

The biggest mistake many organizations make is to assume employees know how to communicate effectively.

It is estimated that as much as 50 percent of our daily communication effort is misunderstood. Therefore, it is essential that we do everything we can to reduce misunderstanding by improving the communication skills of our customer-contact employees. Some points to remember include:

1. Company jargon can be confusing to your customers. Don't use terms such as CRT, ATM, or debit balance.

2. Many words have several meanings, so select your words carefully.

3. Your facial expressions and tone of voice can completely override the words you say.

4. Follow the KISS formula—Keep It Simple, Stupid! Don't be guilty of information overload.

5. Listen carefully and repeat back what you have heard to be sure that you interpreted it correctly.

There's an old saying that bears heeding: "God gave us two ears and one mouth—we're to listen twice as much as we talk!" Just as there are guidelines for talking to customers, so there are rules for effective listening:

1. Be open-minded. Don't fall into the trap of always needing to be right or feeling that everyone is out to prove you are wrong.

2. Make no assumption regarding key points. Always verify the facts of the situation.

3. Don't pass judgment on the speaker before you have listened to what he/she has to say.

4. Concentrate on listening to what the customer is saying. Don't let your mind or your eyes wander.

5. Hear him/her out. Don't jump to conclusions.

Several times over the past few years, I have come across the following story illustrating how distorted our words can become as a result of poor communication.

A colonel issued the following order to his executive officer: "Tomorrow evening at approximately 2000 hours, Halley's Comet will be visible in this area, an event which occurs only once every 75 years. Have the men fall out in the battalion area in fatigues, and I will explain this rare phenomenon to them. In case of rain, we will not be able to see anything, so assemble the men in the theater, and I will show them films of it."

The executive officer passed the order on to the company commander: "By order of the colonel, tomorrow at 2000 hours, Halley's Comet will appear above the battalion area. If it rains, fall the men out in fatigues, then march to the theater where this rare phenomenon will take place, something which occurs only once every 75 years."

Company commander to lieutenant: "By order of the colonel in fatigues at 2000 hours tomorrow evening, the phenomenal Halley's Comet will appear in the theater. In case of rain in the battalion area, the colonel will give another order, something which occurs once every 75 years."

Lieutenant to sergeant: "Tomorrow at 2000 hours, the colonel will appear in the theater with Halley's Comet, something which happens every 75 years. If it rains, the colonel will order the comet into the battalion area."

Sergeant to squad: "When it rains tomorrow at 2000 hours, the phenomenal 75-year-old General Halley, accompanied by the colonel, will drive his comet through the battalion area theater in fatigues."

Just as with the colonel's directives, our words also are often misunderstood. Even worse, often they are repeated to others in a form we would never recognize. So teach your employees to be as brief and precise as possible in their communications with your customers.

Another concept to teach your people is that of psychological stroking. Be aware that such strokes can be both positive and negative. Some examples of positive and negative strokes are:

Positive action strokes

1. Smiling.

2. Offering to help.

3. Shaking his/her hand.

Positive verbal strokes

1. "It's so good to see you today. We've missed you."

2. "You do such a great job."

3. "People definitely like to talk to you."

4. "Hello Mr. _____ ." (use his/her name)

Negative action strokes

1. Continuing to work, ignoring the customer who just walked in.

2. Interrupting the customer.

3. Letting your eyes wander about the room while the customer is talking to you.

Negative verbal strokes

1. "You're so defensive."
2. "It's really not my problem."
3. "Is that the best you can do?"

Obviously, we should strive to make our communication with customers as positive as possible. Monitor your words and actions to see how well you're stroking your customers.

Many books have been written about the importance of body language in our communication with others. The intent here is merely to introduce you to the concept and encourage you to study it further on your own. Here are some clues to watch for:

1. If people cross their arms while you're talking, they could be closing you out.
2. Open hands suggest sincerity and acceptance.
3. It is common for people to cock their heads to one side if what you are saying is of interest to them.
4. Uncertainty is often indicated by touching or rubbing the nose.
5. Wringing the hands often signifies anxiety.
6. People tugging their earlobes may be suggesting they want an opportunity to speak.
7. People who are unsure of themselves, lying, or distorting the truth may cover their mouths with a hand while talking.

An important point to remember is: Don't try to make a decision about a person's feelings or intentions based on just one element of body language. A person's meaning must be read in the context of tone of voice, facial expression, body language, *and* his/her words.

Summary

Nothing is more important to your organization's success than the ability of your people to communicate with customers, each other, and you. There are many elements involved in the communication process—over 90 percent of it via non-verbal channels. Non-verbal communication includes tone of voice, facial expression, and body language.

The biggest mistake many organizations make is to assume employees know how to communicate effectively. The time and money spent training (developing your staff's communication skills) is one of the best investments you'll ever make.

Implementing a Service Strategy   8

Building unrealistic expectations is only the first in a multitude of popular management sins.

A recent newspaper ad for an electric utility company had the following headline in large, bold print:

KNOWLEDGE IS POWER

It caught my attention immediately and, as I considered it, I realized they were only half right. Knowledge is power *only* if it is used and used wisely. If you know all there is to know about service, but just sit in your office, no change or improvement will occur. You have to do something with what you know.

The ideas previously discussed regarding service are not theoretical or complex. On the contrary, most of them are so simple they may be considered to be plain common sense. Even common sense, however, must be acted upon if it is to add value to life and work.

Implementing a service strategy requires that you define what service means for your organization and develop a comprehensive plan for making service a part of daily life for everyone who works for you (that might not be easy). Too often the tendency is to read a few ideas, then immediately try to implement them using a scattergun approach—a little here, a little there.

Example

A delivery company had decided it was time to do something about their image in the community in which they operated. They found that they had no real identity even among their customers. There was nothing unique or special to distinguish them from other companies providing the same type of service.

This company used a variety of vehicles for its pick-up and delivery service. The only identifying mark common to all vehicles was a cardboard sign in the vehicles' side windows with the company name and phone number printed in black on a white, but yellowing, background. Drivers wore whatever they pleased and the outfits ranged from dirty blue jeans and a T-shirt to clean pressed slacks and a dress shirt. Their brochures, letterhead, and statement forms were of different designs, typefaces, and paper stock. The office was always in disarray; it looked like they had just moved in. Nothing about the company was designed to leave a positive, lasting impression. The only thing that kept the company afloat was that their service was above average in spite of everything else. Get the picture?

The owner of the company went to an advertising agency for some suggestions on improving the business' image. After reviewing the situation, the agency suggested a number of things. First they said, "All of your vehicles should be painted the same color, including a nice sign on the sides to identify your company."

The second part of the plan was to gather up samples of all the printed materials they were using, eliminate those items used infrequently, if possible, and redesign those remaining using the same paper, ink color, etc. In other words, all printed materials were to be uniform, to be printed in accordance with predetermined criteria.

Finally, the agency suggested that each employee wear the same color and style of shirt—the beginnings of an employee uniform.

All of these suggestions are good, have value, and will increase the company's visibility. It is important, however, to remember that the second rule (we'll return to rule number one shortly) of implementing change is, *"Go slow. Don't try to change everything at once."* If at all possible, make only one major change at a time so you can evaluate its impact on your business. Otherwise, if you make several changes simultaneously, and your business improves, you won't know which change or changes had the greatest impact.

The delivery company in the example didn't violate the "go slow" rule. They decided to start their image improvement campaign by repainting all of their delivery vehicles as suggested. Do you know what happened? They received the positive recognition they wanted from the public and their customers, but they also learned an important lesson. They had violated the number one rule of change. *"Always communicate to your employees the what and why of what you are planning to do before you do it."*

The painting of the vehicles was done without any communication to the company employees. Their reaction was swift and negative. "Why," they demanded, "are you painting vehicles that already look fine when you could have used the money to pay us more?" This situation definitely placed the business owner in an unenviable position.

Now, compare this situation with the well-planned and executed approach used by Pizza Patrol, a pizza delivery business. Pizza Patrol's owners carefully thought through each detail of the image they wanted to present to the public. For example, all drivers were required to wear military style khaki uniforms complete with the little folding caps. Four-wheel-drive jeeps were used as delivery vehicles. All of the jeeps were white with the Pizza Patrol "wings" insignia and phone number painted on them. To top off the vehicles' appearance, they purchased special license plates for each vehicle that read, HOT 1, HOT 2, HOT 3, etc. All of their signs, advertising, packaging, etc., carried out the patrol image and theme, which is now recognized by virtually everyone in the cities in which they operate. And *they delivered what they promised* because each employee knew the whats and whys of what was being done and their individual role in the plan. Image and service were matched, and the business was a success.

These examples focus primarily on the image or perception presented to the public by these two businesses. Although it is important, image is only one element to be considered in implementing a service strategy. Taking more of a macro view, other factors to be considered in the service improvement process include:

- Customers and their wants, needs, and desires, and their perception of the organization.

- Employees and the degree of their involvement in the process.

- The managers'/owners' commitment to service as a key organizational initiative.

- Suppliers/subcontractors and their understanding of your organization's service goals.

- What the competition is doing in terms of service delivery.

- The long-range objectives of the organization.

Each idea for service improvement should be considered for its potential impact from each of these perspectives.

Understanding your customers has already been discussed in Chapter 3. The key thing to remember is that understanding customers is an ongoing process. You will continually go through the process of understanding your customers, asking them about their preferences, expectations, the level of satisfaction with your service, and what they think of new ideas and proposed changes.

Singles bars usually learn this lesson the hard way. A particular bar will become a favorite of the singles crowd, often for reasons unknown to the owners. Unless the owners take pains to understand what the patrons like about the place and keep in touch with their clientele's frequent changes in taste, in 12 to 15 months this hotspot will be nearly deserted. The crowd will have moved on to the next trendy "in" place.

An entire book could be written on the employees' role in service improvement. First, it is important to recognize and accept the fact that the majority of the problems experienced with employees are self-inflicted. Just think about that for a moment.

I once worked for an organization that built a huge wall between itself and its employees, and that wall had its beginnings in the hiring process. Nearly every manager in the company added his/her share of bricks to the wall, including me. Can you guess what we did wrong? Two things were wrong, and they are closely interrelated.

First, we intentionally hired people who were overqualified because we wanted the "best."

Secondly, we were able to hire overqualified people because we over-promised regarding the future advancement and personal growth opportunities that would be theirs if they took the job. We built false hopes and expectations in the minds and hearts of the people. Sure, some of them were promoted and were given the opportunity to grow professionally, but the majority were not. Therefore, the wall, otherwise known as low morale, came to dominate the organization.

Does this scenario sound familiar? I can't begin to tell you how many times I've heard of this same management error being made in other organizations.

Building unrealistic expectations is only the first in a multitude of popular management sins. What about the inadequate training we often give new employees and limited, if any, cross-training opportunity? *The Wall Street Journal* (March 17, 1987) carried an article with this heading, "IF SERVICE STINKS, why don't companies spend more, a training firm asks." The article went on to say that, despite all the uproar over poor quality of service in the United States, American companies on average are spending only $2.58 per employee to help them improve their ability to service the customer.

Management also is often guilty of what Ken Blanchard, author of *The One-Minute Manager,* calls the leave-alone-zap method of performance feedback. In other words, we wait until they do something wrong and then climb all over them for not doing it correctly.

In a service-oriented environment, employees should be told precisely what is expected of them, what a good job looks like and what to do or who to go to if an extraordinary problem occurs. They should know what criteria is going to be used to evaluate their performance long before their first performance appraisal.

Employees need to be shown that service is a way of managing a business based on customer requirements and expectations. Therefore, a clear, customer-oriented, service system that employees understand, can commit to, and feel a part of is key to implementing a service strategy. In developing your system, keep in mind that it is better to give employees broad, but clear guidelines and let them have some discretionary power in self-management, than to limit their discretionary ability too much.

Be as open as possible with employees about how the organization is doing. Communicate with them early and often regarding anything you've learned from customers and any changes you are planning to make that will affect them. Remind them in as many ways as possible that *nothing happens unless somebody sells something,* so the best way to make the organization successful is to keep the customers happy before *and* after the sale.

The importance of management's commitment to service cannot be overstated. The problem is that the word commitment has been terribly overused but little understood, as have the words quality and excellence.

Recently, I raised the issue of senior management commitment to the president and senior vice president of an insurance company. Their response was, "We really don't want to hear any more about senior management commitment. If we say we are committed to service improvement, that's enough."

To a certain extent, what they said was true. Middle managers and employees will do whatever the person at the top says should be done, but many will doubt the sincerity of the direction given if no action accompanies it. Many will see it as just another management fad or program that will soon fade into the sunset just like all the similar efforts that preceded it.

Lasting service improvement starts with a *demonstration* of commitment (whether you like the word or not is immaterial) at the top levels within the organization—not by edict or proclamation. I realize this idea will not set well with the world's authoritarian managers, but it is true.

How does one demonstrate commitment to service? The secret is to authorize the resources (people, equipment, research, consultant funding, space, etc.) required to get the effort off the ground. Remember, before you make a start in the direction of service improvement, be sure you can follow through and keep the effort going. The worst thing you can do is begin the improvement process and then allow the momentum to fade. Once momentum is lost, double the initial effort will be required to get it moving again.

An excellent example of management demonstrating commitment was found in a medical products company based in Bartlesville, Oklahoma. One of their customers, a hospital, had built a new wing on their facility and had ordered the necessary furniture from this company. The problem was that the hospital had waited to place the order until it was too late to get it to them through normal channels in time for their grand opening. Now it was Friday, and the grand opening was scheduled for the following Monday. Great planning, right? As they say, however, "Where there's a will, there's a way."

The medical products company president authorized his assistant to take a company truck, drive to Tennessee where the furniture manufacturer was located, pick up the needed furniture, and deliver it to the hospital in time for the grand opening. They got the job done and the grand opening was a success.

In the process of making this extraordinary effort to provide superior service, they gained a loyal customer and an invaluable reference, not to mention the example this action set for all the employees of the medical products company.

No discussion of service strategy is complete without dealing with the issue of suppliers/subcontractors. The impact they can have on your business can be significant. Therefore, you should have some means of evaluating their performance because your customers will associate the service received from them with your organization. They become your representatives for better or worse.

Consider the example of the floor covering store I gave in Chapter 1. The store subcontracted the installation of all its products to a third party. A negative reaction stirred within me as soon as the installers arrived to do the job. The two men were unkempt, their vehicle was a rolling junkyard, and their equipment was beat up and dirty. They left after doing a poor job of installing our new kitchen flooring. What kind of image do you suppose I had in my mind regarding the subcontractors *and* the store who had hired them? Because of their carelessness in selecting subcontractors, they lost a customer; I will not buy from that store again.

Most banks selling VISA and MasterCard credit cards offer optional services to their credit card holders in an effort to persuade you to choose their card over that of a competitor. One of the most common services offered is credit card protection. For a small fee, a subcontracting company will keep a list of all of your credit cards and, should they become lost or stolen, the company will take care of notifying the issuers of all your cards for you.

One bank which was subcontracting this service received some complaints from its customers and decided to make test calls to the customer service number given by the card protection company. What they found was surprising. The company's service representatives were slow in answering the phone and were quite unprofessional in the handling of calls.

When notified of the findings, the subcontractor became irate that the bank questioned the quality of their service and had the nerve to make test calls to their representatives. Fortunately for its customers, the bank did not back off on its stance. Rather, they took the time to explain their service philosophy and how they arrived at it, and then informed the subcontractor that the contract with them would not be renewed if they did not comply with certain service standards. In other words, the bank demonstrated commitment to service.

Needless to say, the relationship between the bank and the card protection company was rocky for a while. But, to make a long story short, the subcontractor became convinced of the value of the service standards the bank was proposing, and realized their own company would be better positioned competitively if they made service a major strategic initiative within their organization. Much to their credit, the bank decided to go through this same process with each of its suppliers and subcontractors.

Suppliers and subcontractors are no different than employees when it comes to the issue of service. Unless they know what is expected of them and what your service objectives are, they will probably disappoint you. Worse yet, they may even alienate some of your customers who have become accustomed to the high level of service you normally provide. Service should be discussed before a contract is signed and service performance standards should be a part of all such contracts.

Most companies are at least somewhat aware of what their competition is doing in terms of service. You can never know too much. An excellent example of a company committed to keeping in touch with the competition is given in Tom Peters' and Nancy Austin's book, *A Passion for Excellence*. Remember the example of how Stew Leonard's dairy store seeks feedback from customers given in Chapter 2? Well, here's another tool Stew Leonard uses.

ONE-IDEA CLUB

Stew Leonard (of Stew Leonard's dairy store) solicits his people's ideas regularly. One unique way is via regular visits to competitors. There aren't many stores that compete with Stew across the board, but sometimes he will come across an interesting department like one of his (e.g., bakery goods), or an interesting store in another business (e.g., a florist). When he does, even if it's 300 or 400 miles away, he's likely to grab 15 of his people (including hourly people, even recent new hires) and hop into a 15-person van that he uses for just such occasions.

Off they go to Stew's challenge to join the One-Idea Club. What is the issue? Who will be the first to come up with *one* new idea for Stew's, gleaned from the competitors' outfit? Next, can everyone come up with at least one new idea? (It must be implementable immediately upon returning home.) That's almost all there is to it—but not quite.

Even though Stew Leonard's is at the top of the heap, none of his travelers is allowed to talk about anything that Stew's does better than the competitor they're visiting. The point is for each person to find at least one thing that the competitor does better than Stew's . . . Stew says, "Often as not it'll be a tiny thing. But that's the way *you* get better." The new ideas gleaned are communicated throughout the store in the company newsletter, *Stew's News*.

That illustration is also an excellent example of senior management demonstrating commitment to service. Wouldn't you agree?

Another example of a less elaborate approach that was just as effective is that related by a bookstore owner in California. This owner was new to the business and so relied heavily on friends and visits to other bookstores for ideas. It was the visits to competitors that helped him determine that his magazine display should be visible to people passing by the front of the store rather than at the back of the store. Why? Magazines are a good "draw" to get people into the store, so you want to be sure they can see that you stock them. Obviously, once the customers are in the store, they will be more likely to buy books as well. In this case, moving the magazines from the back to the front of the store resulted in a dramatic increase in magazine sales and subsequently, book sales increased as well.

Remember, it's the little things that can mean the difference between success and failure for your organization. So, when you're shopping your competition, don't look only for big ideas, pay attention to the tiniest of details as well.

The final factor to be considered in implementing a service strategy is the organization's long-range objective. First, you must be clear on what the one, overriding long-range objective of your organization is. You must be able to answer the questions:

1. What do we want our organization to be?

2. What is its nature and purpose?

3. Where should it be headed?

4. What is our vision of what it should become?

The tendency for most is to gloss over such questions and assume we know what we want and how to get there.

Don't confuse the idea of a long-range objective with planning. These are two distinct facets of management responsibility critical to the success of any organization. But the objective is *what* the organization wants to be, and the plan is *how* to get there—the actual operational steps required.

By now, you're probably asking what in the world this has to do with service strategy. The answer is quite simple.

Your key long-range objective determines what products or services you decide to offer, how they will be marketed, the allocation of your organization's resources, and how you want to position your organization in the eyes of the public—all of which are directly related to service delivery. For example, you might only want to carry products with a certain minimum warranty, or products you can service so you can personally guarantee service in your advertising and marketing efforts. Expanding your product line into what is a new area for your organization requires that you commit the resources—time, money, people, training— required to make your people knowledgeable and capable of dealing with customers' inquiries and handling problems that arise regarding the new product.

Developing a solid statement of your key long-range objective allows you to evaluate each decision facing your organization in light of what is most important to you. It serves as a framework upon which your organization will be built and will help you think through the service requirements associated with current and proposed products.

Summary

Implementation of an effective service strategy is not painless and cannot be done overnight. Several steps are required, and skipping any one of them can lead to problems.

1. First and foremost, communicate what you are doing in each step to your employees. They must feel they are a part of the service improvement effort from the very beginning. After all, it is the employees who will do the actual implementation.

2. Define in a clear, concise mission statement what you think service means for your organization, and develop a means of regularly measuring and reporting

how well the organization is meeting your definition of service.

3. Get feedback directly from your customers regarding their wants, needs, and desires, and their perception of your organization.

4. Involve your employees. Ask them how service can be improved. Tell them *exactly* what you expect of them and why. Share what you found out from your customers with them.

5. Demonstrate top management commitment to service improvement by allocating the resources needed to respond to issues raised by customers and employees, and by acknowledging and rewarding actionable employee suggestions.

6. Share your service mission statement and service philosophy with your suppliers and subcontractors and let them know exactly what you expect of them so there are no surprises. Evaluate them on a regular basis just as you do your own employees. Those that are worth doing business with will appreciate your input.

7. Stay current with what your competition is doing. Pay attention to the little things. Service is doing hundreds of little things well.

8. Evaluate all new products within the framework of your company's overriding long-range objective, and determine what you will need to do to provide the service that customers expect with the new product.

9. Constantly question the status quo. Always ask, "How can we do it better?"

The underlying message in all this is, integrate your improvement efforts into a meaningful, planned approach. Target them carefully—don't shotgun.

Making service a regular part of daily life for all your people might require several years depending on your organization's size and complexity. The 3M Company suggests there are five stages that must be passed through before quality becomes an integral part of the organizational woodwork. I would suggest these same stages can be adapted to institutionalization of service.

1. *Knowledge.* Must be aware of what service means for the organization and the customer, and how to develop an improvement plan.

2. *Courage.* Senior management must be willing to take the first step by demonstrating commitment to the improvement process through allocation of required resources.

3. *Acceptable.* The new philosophy of service must be presented to employees and middle management in such a way that they are willing to give the proposed improvement plan a fair shot. Senior management must be willing to move slowly at first.

4. *Normative.* The new service philosophy becomes the rule rather than the exception. The improvement process gains momentum.

5. *Value.* Everyone in the organization is thoroughly convinced of the validity of service as a competitive weapon. Service permeates all discussions and decisions within the organization.

Whether you have one employee or 100,000 employees, the process of implementing a service strategy is the same. The challenge for each organization lies in how well its people can adapt the nine implementation steps to their specific situation. If you have the patience and courage to shepherd your people through the entire process, the results will more than justify the effort.

EPILOGUE

The time is now. Everything you need to help you develop and implement a successful service strategy is available to you if you're willing to do a little work. As small as it might be, take the first step and remember the old Chinese proverb, "A journey of a thousand miles begins with the first step." The journey won't be easy, and it won't be painless—success never is.

BIBLIOGRAPHY

Albrecht, Karl, and Ronald E. Zemke. *Service America*. Homewood, IL.: Dow Jones-Irwin, 1985.

Naisbitt, John. *Megatrends*. New York: Warner Books, Inc., 1982.

Phillips, Michael, and Salli Rasberry. *Honest Business*. New York: Random House, 1981.

Townsend, Patrick L. *Commit to Quality*. New York: John Wiley & Sons, Inc., 1986.

Tregoe, Benjamin B., and John W. Zimmerman. *Top Management Strategy*. New York: Touchstone, 1980.

Tregoe, Benjamin B., John W. Zimmerman, Ronald A. Smith, and Peter M. Tobia. *Vision in Action*. New York: Simon and Schuster, 1989.

Walton, Mary. *The Deming Management Method*. New York: Dodd, Mead & Company, 1986.

Index